TAKE TIME FOR Joy

A photographic journey to fill your year with 365 days of inspiration

Mac Anderson AND Todd AND Brad Reed

simple ▶ truths
small books. BIG IMPACT.

Photo Credits
Cover and internals images © Todd and Brad Reed Photography

Published by Simple Truths, an imprint of Sourcebooks, Inc.
P.O. Box 4410, Naperville, Illinois 60567-4410
(630) 961-3900
Fax: (630) 961-2168
www.sourcebooks.com

Printed and bound in China.
QL 10 9 8 7 6 5 4 3 2 1

INTRODUCTION

Life, at times, can be a treadmill. We keep running and telling ourselves that we'll slow down someday soon. We'll stop to take time for ourselves, for our family, or to smell the roses. Or, in other words, to take time for joy!

That's what this beautiful book is all about: a gentle reminder that life is not always about being better or best. Sometimes it is about *just being!*

It's about being in the moment, to truly capture the joy of that moment.

Ever since I was a freshman in college, I've loved quotations. The right words can engage the brain and bring an idea to life...or capture the joy of living. With quotes, I've had many "aha" moments where I've read them and thought, *Wow, that's exactly how I feel!*

In *Take Time for Joy*, I'm sharing 365 of my favorite quotes to inspire you, to make you think, and occasionally to make you laugh. Each quote is intended to bring a "shot of joy" into your daily life!

What makes this book extra special is not only the quotes, but also the beautiful photographs by Todd and Brad Reed. In my years at Successories, and now at Simple Truths, I have seen the work of many of the world's top nature photographers, and I can say with conviction that Todd and Brad are two of the best.

The combination of inspirational, joyful, and humorous quotes paired with award-winning photography makes this beautiful coffee-table book a one-of-a-kind treasure.

I hope you will keep it close and read it often. Make it a constant source of joy and inspiration! And just one more thing—share it with those you love.

To life and the joy it brings,

Mac Anderson
Founder, Simple Truths

Take Time for JOY...
Every Day of Your Life

JANUARY 1

Joy is not in things; it is in us.

—*Richard Wagner*

JANUARY 2

I praise loudly; I blame softly.

—*Catherine II*

JANUARY 3

Real joy comes not from ease or riches or from the praise of men, but from doing something worthwhile.

—*Sir Wilfred Grenfell*

JANUARY 4

Life isn't about finding yourself. Life is about creating yourself.

—*George Bernard Shaw*

JANUARY 5

The joy of a spirit is the measure of its power.

—*Ninon de l'Enclos*

JANUARY 6

A good head and a good heart are always a formidable combination.

—*Nelson Mandela*

JANUARY 7

Don't take life too seriously. You will never get out of it alive.

—*Elbert Hubbard*

JANUARY 8

Constant kindness can accomplish much. As the sun makes ice melt, kindness causes misunderstanding, mistrust, and hostility to evaporate.

—*Albert Schweitzer*

JANUARY 9

To find joy in work is to discover the fountain of YOUTH.

—*Pearl S. Buck*

JANUARY 10

You will never experience the earth with all its wonders in this time again. Don't wait for one last look at the ocean, the sky, the stars, or a loved one. Go look now.

—*Elisabeth Kübler-Ross*

JANUARY 11

Laughter is the best medicine for a long and happy life. He who laughs—lasts!

—*Wilford A. Peterson*

JANUARY 12

Plenty of people miss their share of happiness, not because they never found it, but because they didn't stop to enjoy it.

—*William Feather*

JANUARY 13

True greatness is firmly rooted in humility.

—Ralph Marston

JANUARY 14

Things turn out best for the people who make the best of the way things turn out.

—John Wooden

JANUARY 15

The human race has only one really effective weapon and that is laughter. The moment it arises, all your irritations and resentments slip away, and the sunny spirit takes their place.

—Mark Twain

JANUARY 16

Weather forecast for tonight: dark. Continued dark overnight, with widely scattered light by morning.

—*George Carlin*

JANUARY 17

Sometimes your joy is the source of your smile, but sometimes your smile can be the source of your joy.

—*Thích Nhất Hanh*

JANUARY 18

A good laugh and a long sleep are the two best cures for anything.

—*Irish Proverb*

JANUARY 19

There are those who give with joy, and that joy is their reward.

—*Kahlil Gibran*

JANUARY 20

If you want to be happy, be.

—*Leo Tolstoy*

JANUARY 21

Happiness is not something ready-made. It comes from your own actions.

—*Dalai Lama*

JANUARY 22

Happiness often sneaks in through a door you didn't know you left open.

—*John Barrymore*

JANUARY 23

Never lose an opportunity of seeing anything that is BEAUTIFUL...
Welcome it in every face, in every fair sky, in every fair flower.

—*Ralph Waldo Emerson*

JANUARY 24

It is never too late to be what you might have been.

—George Eliot

JANUARY 25

Worry is like rocking in a rocking chair: it gives you something to do but never gets you anywhere.

—Erma Bombeck

JANUARY 26

There is no passion to be found playing small—in settling for a life that is less than the one you are capable of living.

—Nelson Mandela

JANUARY 27

All the flowers of all the tomorrows are in the seeds of today.

—Proverb

JANUARY 28

What really matters is what you do with what you have.

—H. G. Wells

JANUARY 29

There is no greater joy nor greater reward than to make a fundamental difference in someone's life.

—Sister Mary Rose McGeady

JANUARY 30

True happiness comes from the joy of deeds well done, the zest of creating things new.

—Antoine de Saint-Exupéry

JANUARY 31

If you risk nothing, then you risk everything.

—Geena Davis

FEBRUARY 1

Change always comes bearing GIFTS.

—*Price Pritchett*

FEBRUARY 2

Let a joy keep you. Reach out your hands and take it when it runs by.

—*Carl Sandburg*

FEBRUARY 3

Happiness is having a scratch for every itch.

—*Ogden Nash*

FEBRUARY 4

Happiness cannot come from without. It must come from within.

—*Helen Keller*

FEBRUARY 5

The art of being wise is knowing what to overlook.

—*William James*

FEBRUARY 6

We hope that, when the insects take over the world, they will remember with gratitude how we took them along on all our picnics.

—Bill Vaughan

FEBRUARY 7

When your heart speaks, take good notes.

—Judith Campbell

FEBRUARY 8

Before I got married I had six theories about bringing up children; now I have six children and no theories.

—John Wilmot

FEBRUARY 9

Laughter is a tranquilizer with no side effects.

—Arnold H. Glasow

FEBRUARY 10

A person who never made a mistake never tried anything NEW.

—*Albert Einstein*

FEBRUARY 11

What soap is to the body, laughter is to the soul.

—Yiddish Proverb

FEBRUARY 12

He that falls in love with himself will have no rivals.

—Benjamin Franklin

FEBRUARY 13

Joy is the feeling of grinning inside.

—Melba Colgrove

FEBRUARY 14

Far away there in the sunshine are my highest aspirations. I may not reach them, but I can look up and see their beauty, believe in them, and try to follow where they lead.

—*Louisa May Alcott*

FEBRUARY 15

It is not how much we have, but how much we enjoy, that makes happiness.

—*Charles Spurgeon*

FEBRUARY 16

The future depends on what we do in the present.

—Mahatma Gandhi

FEBRUARY 17

The time to be happy is now. The place to be happy is here. The way to be happy is to make others so.

—Robert G. Ingersoll

FEBRUARY 18

It is one of the most beautiful compensations of life that no man can sincerely try to help another without helping himself.

—Ralph Waldo Emerson

Imagination is the highest kite one can FLY.

—*Lauren Bacall*

FEBRUARY 20

Create the highest, grandest vision possible for your life, because you become what you believe.

—Oprah Winfrey

FEBRUARY 21

Change your thoughts and you change your world.

—Norman Vincent Peale

FEBRUARY 22

Look at everything as though you are seeing it for the first time, with eyes of a child, fresh with wonder.

—Joseph Cornell

FEBRUARY 23

Let us always meet each other with a smile, for the smile is the beginning of 𝒬ove.

—*Mother Teresa*

FEBRUARY 24

Cleaning your house while your kids are still growing is like shoveling the walk before it stops snowing.

—*Phyllis Diller*

FEBRUARY 25

Keep your face to the sunshine and you cannot see a shadow.

—*Helen Keller*

FEBRUARY 26

By being yourself, you put something wonderful in the world that was not there before.

—*Edwin Elliot*

FEBRUARY 27

The heart that gives, gathers.

—*Marianne Moore*

FEBRUARY 28

It was only a sunny smile, and little it cost in the giving, but like morning light it scattered the night and made the day worth living.

—*F. Scott Fitzgerald*

MARCH 1

Laughter is an instant vacation.

—Milton Berle

MARCH 2

In dreams and in love there are no impossibilities.

—*János Arany*

MARCH 3

Enjoy the little things, for one day you may look back and realize they were the big things.

—*Robert Brault*

MARCH 4

How simple it is to see that all the worry in the world cannot control the future. How simple it is to see that we can only be happy now. And that there will never be a time when it is not now.

—*Gerald G. Jampolsky*

MARCH 5

When angry, count to ten before you speak; if very angry, count to one hundred.

—*Thomas Jefferson*

MARCH 6

Most folks are as happy as they make up their minds to be.

—*Abraham Lincoln*

MARCH 7

To love and be loved is to feel the sun from both sides.

—*David Viscott*

MARCH 8

Happiness is as a butterfly, which when pursued, is always just beyond your grasp, but which, if you will sit down quietly, may alight upon you.

—*Nathaniel Hawthorne*

MARCH 9

Your attitude, not your aptitude,
will determine your altitude.

—*Zig Ziglar*

MARCH 10

No act of kindness, no matter how small, is ever wasted.

—*Aesop*

MARCH 11

When we choose not to focus on what is missing
from our lives but are grateful for the abundance
that's present...we experience heaven on earth.

—*Sarah Ban Breathnach*

MARCH 12

To succeed in life, you need three things: a
wishbone, a backbone, and a funny bone.

—*Reba McEntire*

MARCH 13

Our greatest danger in life is in permitting the urgent things to crowd out the important.

—*Charles E. Hummel*

MARCH 14

Love doesn't make the world go 'round. Love is what makes the ride worthwhile.

—*Franklin P. Jones*

MARCH 15

Your vision will become clear only when you look into your heart. Who looks outside, dreams. Who looks inside, awakens.

—*Carl Jung*

MARCH 16

I dwell in Possibility.

—*Emily Dickinson*

MARCH 17

The best thing to hold onto in life is each other.

—*Audrey Hepburn*

MARCH 18

The bad news is time flies. The good news is you're the pilot.

—*Michael Altshuler*

MARCH 19

We have committed the Golden Rule to memory; let us now commit it to life.

—*Edwin Markham*

MARCH 20

I am a great believer in luck, and I find the harder I work, the more I have of it.

—*Thomas Jefferson*

MARCH 21

Sometimes our light goes out, but is blown
again into instant flame by an ENCOUNTER
with another human being.

—*Albert Schweitzer*

MARCH 22

If at first you don't succeed…so much for skydiving.

—Henny Youngman

MARCH 23

Never underestimate the power of dreams and the influence of the human spirit.

—Wilma Rudolph

MARCH 24

The best and most beautiful things in life cannot be seen or even touched—they must be felt with the heart.

—Helen Keller

MARCH 25

Hope arouses, as nothing else can arouse, a passion for the possible.

—William Sloane Coffin

MARCH 26

To get the full value of joy, you must have someone to divide it with.

—*Mark Twain*

MARCH 27

Give to the world the best you have and the best will come back to you.

—*Madeline S. Bridges*

MARCH 28

To love what you do and feel that it matters, how could anything be more fun?

—*Katharine Graham*

MARCH 29

You can have everything in life you want if you will just help enough other people get what they want.

—Zig Ziglar

MARCH 30

A single act of kindness throws out roots in all directions, and the roots spring up and make new trees.

—Amelia Earhart

MARCH 31

Wake up with a smile and go after life...
Live it, enjoy it, taste it, smell it, feel it.

—Joe Knapp

The best time to give advice to your children is while they're still young enough to BELIEVE you know what you're talking about.

—Evan Esar

In the long run, we shape our lives, and we shape ourselves. The process never ends until we die. And the choices we make are ultimately our own responsibility.

—Eleanor Roosevelt

Behind me is infinite power. Before me is endless possibility. Around me is boundless opportunity. Why should I fear?

—Stella Stuart

There is joy in work. There is no happiness except in the realization that we have accomplished something.

—Henry Ford

APRIL 5

The heart has reasons that reason cannot know.

—*Blaise Pascal*

APRIL 6

What lies behind us and what lies before us are tiny matters compared to what lies within us.

—*Ralph Waldo Emerson*

APRIL 7

Our attitude toward life determines life's attitude toward us.

—*John N. Mitchell*

APRIL 8

To dream anything that you want to dream. That is the beauty of the human mind. To do anything that you want to do. That is the strength of the human will. To trust yourself to test your limits. That is the courage to succeed.

—Bernard Edmonds

APRIL 9

Only passions, great passions, can elevate the soul to great things.

—Denis Diderot

APRIL 10

The real voyage of discovery consists not in seeking new landscapes, but in having new eyes.

—Marcel Proust

APRIL 11

Now and then it's good to pause in the pursuit of happiness and just be HAPPY.

—*Guillaume Apollinaire*

APRIL 12

Life is made of memorable moments. We must teach ourselves to really live...to love the journey not the destination.

—Ann Quindlen

APRIL 13

All you need is love. But a little chocolate now and then doesn't hurt.

—Charles M. Schulz

APRIL 14

Life is an echo. What you send out comes back.

—Zig Ziglar

APRIL 15

Three grand essentials to happiness in this life are something to do, something to love, and something to hope for.

—*Joseph Addison*

APRIL 16

Purpose and laughter are the twins that must not separate. Each is empty without the other.

—*Robert K. Greenleaf*

APRIL 17

Laughter is the shock absorber that eases the blows of life.

—*Unknown*

The purpose of our lives is to **GIVE** birth to the best which is within us.

—*Marianne Williamson*

APRIL 19

The most powerful weapon on earth is the human soul on fire.

—*Ferdinand Foch*

APRIL 20

Cherish your visions and your dreams as they are the children of your soul, the blueprints of your ultimate achievements.

—*Napoleon Hill*

APRIL 21

To be what we are, and to become what we are capable of becoming, is the only end of life.

—*Robert Louis Stevenson*

APRIL 22

Trust yourself. Create the kind of self that you will be happy to live with all your life. Make the most of yourself by fanning the tiny, inner sparks of possibility into flames of achievement.

—*Golda Meir*

APRIL 23

Happiness is a direction, not a place.

—*Sydney J. Harris*

APRIL 24

We act as though comfort and luxury were the chief requirements of life, when all that we need to make us really happy is something to be enthusiastic about.

—*Charles Kingsley*

APRIL 25

Swing hard, in case they throw the ball where you're swinging.

—Duke Snider

APRIL 26

Choose a job you love, and you will never have to work a day in your life.

—Confucius

APRIL 27

The here and now is all we have, and if we play it right it's all we'll need.

—Ann Richards

Happiness lies in the joy of achievement and the thrill of creative effort.

—*Franklin D. Roosevelt*

There is a time to let things happen and a time to make things happen.

—*Hugh Prather*

Every thought is a seed. If you plant crab apples, don't count on harvesting Golden Delicious.

—*Bill Meyer*

No kind action ever stops with itself.
One kind action leads to ANOTHER.
Good example is followed.

—*Amelia Earhart*

MAY 2

The miracle is this: the more we share, the more we have.

—*Leonard Nimoy*

MAY 3

A sense of humor...is needed armor. Joy in one's heart and some laughter on one's lips is a sign that the person down deep has a pretty good grasp of life.

—*Hugh Sidey*

MAY 4

Don't wait around for other people to be happy for you. Any happiness you get you've got to make yourself.

—*Alice Walker*

MAY 5

Few things in the world are more powerful than a positive push. A smile. A word of optimism and hope. A "you can do it!" when things are tough.

—*Richard M. DeVos*

MAY 6

From small beginnings come great things.

—*Proverb*

MAY 7

The true meaning of life is to plant trees under whose shade you do not expect to sit.

—*Nelson Henderson*

MAY 8

Enthusiasm is nothing more or less than faith in action.

—*Henry Chester*

MAY 9

Your future depends on many things, but mostly on **you.**

—*Frank Tyger*

MAY 10

Throw your heart over the fence and the rest will follow.

—*Norman Vincent Peale*

MAY 11

A happy family is but an earlier heaven.

—*George Bernard Shaw*

MAY 12

A man travels the world over in search of what he needs and returns home to find it.

—*George Moore*

MAY 13

Do something wonderful, people may imitate it.

—*Albert Schweitzer*

MAY 14

Nothing happens unless first a dream.

—*Carl Sandburg*

MAY 15

When you get the chance to sit it out or dance, I hope you dance. I hope you dance.

—*Lee Ann Womack*

MAY 16

Life engenders life. Energy creates energy. It is by spending oneself that one becomes rich.

—*Sarah Bernhardt*

MAY 17

You can't live a perfect day without doing something for someone who will never be able to repay you.

—*John Wooden*

MAY 18

Person to person, moment to moment, as we love, we change the world.

—*Samahria Lyte Kaufman*

MAY 19

Against the assault of laughter nothing can stand.

—*Mark Twain*

MAY 20

Life expectancy would grow by leaps and bounds if green vegetables smelled as good as bacon.

—*Doug Larson*

MAY 21

For happiness one needs security, but joy can spring like a flower even from the cliffs of despair.

—*Anne Morrow Lindbergh*

MAY 22

I intend to live forever. So far, so good.

—*Steven Wright*

MAY 23

Our brightest blazes of gladness are commonly kindled by unexpected sparks.

—*Samuel Johnson*

MAY 24

The happiest people are those who do the most for others.

—*Booker T. Washington*

MAY 25

Beauty is whatever gives joy.

—*Edna St. Vincent Millay*

MAY 26

The sun does not shine for a few trees and flowers, but for the wide world's joy.

—*Henry Ward Beecher*

MAY 27

You can't be a smart cookie if you have a crummy attitude.

—*John C. Maxwell*

MAY 28

Thousands of candles can be lighted from a single candle, and the life of the candle will not be shortened. Happiness never decreases by being shared.

—*Gautama Buddha*

MAY 29

What we have once enjoyed we can never lose. All that we love deeply becomes a part of us.

—*Helen Keller*

MAY 30

It's not where you start— it's where you finish that counts.

—*Zig Ziglar*

MAY 31

Seek to do good, and you will find that happiness will run after you.

—*James Freeman Clarke*

JUNE

JUNE 1

Don't limit yourself. Many people limit themselves to what they think they can do. You can go as far as your mind lets you. What you believe, remember, you can ACHIEVE.

—*Mary Kay Ash*

71

JUNE 2

Remember, happiness doesn't depend upon who you are or what you have; it depends solely upon what you think.

—*Dale Carnegie*

JUNE 3

You must be the change you wish to see in the world.

—*Mahatma Gandhi*

JUNE 4

All my life through, the new sights of Nature made me rejoice like a child.

—*Marie Curie*

JUNE 5

Optimism is the faith that leads to achievement. Nothing can be done without hope and confidence.

—*Helen Keller*

JUNE 6

If one advances confidently in the direction of his dreams, and endeavors to live the life which he has imagined, he will meet with success unexpected in common hours.

—*Henry David Thoreau*

JUNE 7

A person can succeed at almost anything for which he has unlimited enthusiasm.

—*Charles Schwab*

JUNE 8

A sense of humor snuffs out our sparks of friction before they get to our fuel tank.

—*Fred Smith*

JUNE 9

We shall never know all the good that a simple smile can do.

—*Mother Teresa*

JUNE 10

Love is life. And if you miss love, you miss life.

—*Leo Buscaglia*

JUNE 11

There are two ways of spreading light: to be the candle or the mirror that reflects it.

—*Edith Wharton*

JUNE 12

Happiness is a conscious choice, not an automatic RESPONSE.

—*Mildred Barthel*

Regardless of your lot in life, you can build something beautiful on it.

—*Zig Ziglar*

A dream doesn't become reality through magic; it takes sweat, determination, and hard work.

—*Colin Powell*

If you don't think every day is a good day, just try missing one.

—*Cavett Robert*

JUNE 16

Courage doesn't always roar. Sometimes courage is the quiet voice at the end of the day, saying, "I will try again tomorrow."

—*Mary Anne Radmacher*

JUNE 17

A well-developed sense of humor is the pole that adds balance to your steps as you walk the tightrope of life.

—*William Arthur Ward*

At the end of your life, you will never regret not having passed one more test, not winning one more verdict, or not closing one more deal. You will regret time not spent with a husband, a child, a friend, or a parent.

—*Barbara Bush*

Joy in looking and comprehending is nature's most beautiful gift.

—*Albert Einstein*

Wherever you go, go there with all your heart.

—*Confucius*

JUNE 21

A thing of beauty is a joy forever:
its loveliness increases; it will
never pass into nothingness.

—*John Keats*

Happiness is not in our circumstances but in ourselves. It is not something we see, like a rainbow, or feel, like the heat of a fire. HAPPINESS is something we are.

—*John B. Sheerin*

JUNE 23

Remember that the happiest people are not those getting more, but those giving more.

—*H. Jackson Brown Jr.*

JUNE 24

Joy is prayer—Joy is strength—Joy is love—Joy is a net of love by which you can catch souls.

—*Mother Teresa*

JUNE 25

There are souls in this world which have the gift of finding joy everywhere and of leaving it behind them when they go.

—*Frederick Faber*

Never doubt that a small group of thoughtful, committed citizens can change the world. Indeed, it is the only thing that ever has.

—*Margaret Mead*

Those who bring sunshine into the lives of others cannot keep it from themselves.

—*James M. Barrie*

To the world you may be just one person, but to one person you may be the world.

—*Brandi Snyder*

JUNE 29

Carry out a random act of kindness, with no expectation of reward, safe in the knowledge that one day someone might do the same for you.

—*Princess Diana*

JUNE 30

To give without any reward, or any notice, has a special quality of its own.

—*Anne Morrow Lindbergh*

JULY 1

When you learn, teach.
When you get, GIVE.

—*Maya Angelou*

JULY 2

If you love something, set it free. Unless it's chocolate. Never release chocolate.

—*Renee Duvall*

JULY 3

A kind heart is a fountain of gladness, making everything in its vicinity freshen into smiles.

—*Washington Irving*

JULY 4

For attractive lips, speak words of kindness. For lovely eyes, seek out the good in people... For poise, walk with the knowledge that you never walk alone.

—*Sam Levenson*

JULY 5

Focus on the journey, not the destination. Joy is found not in finishing an activity but in doing it.

—*Greg Anderson*

JULY 6

May you remember that love flows best when it flows freely, and it is in giving that we receive the greatest gift.

—*Kate Nowak*

JULY 7

Wisdom is knowing the right path to take... Integrity is taking it.

—*M. H. McKee*

I expect to pass through this world but once. Any good therefore that I can do, or any kindness or abilities that I can show to any fellow creature, let me do it now. Let me not defer it or neglect it, for I shall not pass this way again.

—*William Penn*

Kind words are a creative force, a power that concurs in the building up of all that is good, and energy that showers blessings upon the world.

—*Lawrence G. Lovasik*

JULY 10

Life is short and we have never too much time for gladdening the hearts of those who are traveling the dark journey with us. Oh, be swift to love! Make haste to be KIND.

—*Henri-Frédéric Amiel*

It is neither wealth nor splendor, but tranquility and occupation which give you happiness.

—*Thomas Jefferson*

A bird doesn't sing because it has an answer. It sings because it has a song.

—*Chinese Proverb*

We tend to forget that happiness doesn't come as a result of getting something we don't have, but rather of recognizing and appreciating what we do have.

—*Frederick Koenig*

JULY 14

All that is required to feel that here and now is happiness is a simple, frugal heart.

—*Nikos Kazantzakis*

JULY 15

You have succeeded in life when all you really want is only what you really need.

—*Vernon Howard*

JULY 16

He who obtains has little. He who scatters has much.

—*Lao Tzu*

JULY 17

There is only one happiness in this life, to love and be loved.

—*George Sand*

One word frees us of all
the weight and pain of life:
that word is LOVE.

—Sophocles

JULY 19

Celebrate the happiness that friends are always giving.
Make every day a holiday and celebrate just living!

—*Amanda Bradley*

JULY 20

I've learned that people will forget what you said,
people will forget what you did, but people will never
forget how you made them feel.

—*Maya Angelou*

JULY 21

The purpose of human life is to serve, and to show
compassion and the will to help others.

—*Albert Schweitzer*

JULY 22

You know you are old when you have lost all your marvels.

—*Mary Browne*

JULY 23

What we have done for ourselves alone dies with us;
what we have done for others and the world remains
and is immortal.

—*Albert Pike*

JULY 24

Live your life each day as you would climb a mountain.
An occasional glance toward the summit keeps the goal in
mind, but many beautiful scenes are to be observed from
each new vantage point. Climb slowly, steadily, enjoying
each passing moment; and the view from the summit will
serve as a fitting climax for the journey.

—*Harold V. Melchert*

JULY 25

Be happy. It's one way of being wise.

—Sidonie Gabrielle Colette

JULY 26

The person who knows how to laugh at himself will never cease to be amused.

—Shirley MacLaine

JULY 27

There is only one way to happiness and that is to cease worrying about things which are beyond the power of our will.

—Epictetus

JULY 28

Wisdom begins in wonder.

—Socrates

JULY 29

In nature, nothing is perfect and everything is perfect. Trees can be contorted, bent in weird ways, and they're still beautiful.

—Alice Walker

JULY 30

Being happy doesn't mean that everything is perfect. It means that you've decided to look beyond the imperfections.

—Gerard Way

JULY 31

If you carry joy in your life,
you can heal any ♀MOMENT.

—*Carlos Santana*

AUGUST 1

Live in the present moment and find your interest and happiness in the things of TODAY.

—*Emmett Fox*

AUGUST 2

Set peace of mind as your highest goal, and organize your life around it.

—Brian Tracy

AUGUST 3

The walls we build around us to keep sadness out also keep out the joy.

—Jim Rohn

AUGUST 4

Happiness comes only when we push our brains and hearts to the farthest reaches of which we are capable.

—Leo Rosten

AUGUST 5

Destiny is not a matter of chance; it is a matter of choice. It is not a thing to be waited for; it is a thing to be achieved.

—William Jennings Bryan

AUGUST 6

The only thing that stands between a man and what he wants from life is often merely the will to try it and the faith to believe that it is possible.

—David Viscott

AUGUST 7

It's a funny thing about life; if you refuse to accept anything but the best, you very often get it.

—W. Somerset Maugham

AUGUST 8

Nothing can bring you happiness but yourself.

—*Ralph Waldo Emerson*

AUGUST 9

First we make our attitudes. Then our attitudes make us.

—*Denis Waitley*

AUGUST 10

Service is the rent we pay for being. It is the very purpose of life, and not something you do in your spare time.

—*Marian Wright Edelman*

AUGUST 11

Laughter is sunshine in any LIFE.

—*William Thackeray*

AUGUST 12

Joy is the simplest form of gratitude.

—Karl Barth

AUGUST 13

But as the most beautiful light is born of darkness, so the faith that springs from conflict is often the strongest and best.

—R. Turnbull

AUGUST 14

Life must be lived as play.

—Plato

AUGUST 15

When opportunity knocks, some people are in the backyard looking for four-leaf clovers.

—Polish Proverb

AUGUST 16

Everyone chases after happiness, not noticing that happiness is right at their heels.

—*Bertolt Brecht*

AUGUST 17

To accomplish great things, we must not only act, but also dream; not only plan, but also believe.

—*Anatole France*

AUGUST 18

If you want to lift yourself up, lift up someone else.

—*Booker T. Washington*

AUGUST 19

Earth LAUGHS
in flowers.

—*Ralph Waldo Emerson*

AUGUST 20

Research has shown that the best way to be happy is to make each day happy.

—*Deepak Chopra*

AUGUST 21

For it is in giving that we receive.

—*Saint Francis of Assisi*

AUGUST 22

Today, see if you can stretch your heart and expand your love so that it touches not only those to whom you can give it easily, but also to those who need it so much.

—*Daphne Rose Kingma*

You give but little when you give
of your possessions. It is when you
give of yourself that you truly give.

—*Kahlil Gibran*

AUGUST 24

The one-a-day vitamin for the soul is helping another person.

—*Stephen Post*

AUGUST 25

We gain strength, and courage, and confidence by each experience in which we really stop to look fear in the face... We must do that which we think we cannot.

—*Eleanor Roosevelt*

Acts of love are what will bring peace to your life and to the world.

—*Dr. Lee Jampolsky*

I have found that among its other benefits, giving liberates the soul of the giver.

—*Maya Angelou*

There is no happiness in having or getting, but only in giving.

—*Henry Drummond*

AUGUST 29

You never know when one kind act, or one word of encouragement, can change a life forever.

—Zig Ziglar

AUGUST 30

There is no condition, no circumstance, no problem that love cannot solve. Love, for yourself and others, is always the solution.

—Neale Donald Walsch

AUGUST 31

The best portion of a good man's life: his little, nameless, unremembered acts of kindness and love.

—William Wordsworth

SEPTEMBER 1

Gratitude is the fairest blossom which springs from the S**O**UL.

—*Henry Ward Beecher*

SEPTEMBER 2

People who live the most fulfilling lives are the ones who are always rejoicing at what they have.

—Richard Carlson

SEPTEMBER 3

Let us be grateful to the people who make us happy; they are the charming gardeners who make our souls blossom.

—Marcel Proust

SEPTEMBER 4

A laugh, to be joyous, must flow from a joyous heart, for without kindness, there can be no true joy.

—Thomas Carlyle

SEPTEMBER 5

We can only be said to be alive in those moments when our hearts are conscious of our treasures.

—*Thorton Wilder*

SEPTEMBER 6

A heart needs only its own voice to do what is right.

—*Vanna Bonta*

SEPTEMBER 7

There are only two ways to live your life. One is as though nothing is a miracle. The other is as though everything is a miracle.

—*Albert Einstein*

A warm smile is the universal language of kindness.

—*William Arthur Ward*

There is more to life than increasing its speed.

—*Mahatma Gandhi*

Today, give a stranger one of your smiles. It might be the only sunshine he sees all day.

—*H. Jackson Brown Jr.*

SEPTEMBER 11

As we work to create light for others, we naturally light our own WAY.

—*Mary Anne Radmacher*

SEPTEMBER 12

Never lose a chance of saying a kind word.

—*William Makepeace Thackeray*

SEPTEMBER 13

Joy is what happens to us when we allow ourselves to recognize how good things really are.

—*Marianne Williamson*

SEPTEMBER 14

The best way to predict your future is to create it.

—*Abraham Lincoln*

SEPTEMBER

SEPTEMBER 15

The love we give away is the only love we keep.

—*Elbert Hubbard*

SEPTEMBER 16

Rules for happiness: something to do,
someone to love, something to hope for.

—*Immanuel Kant*

SEPTEMBER 17

You will rise by lifting others.

—*Robert G. Ingersoll*

SEPTEMBER 18

The meaning of life is to find your gift. The purpose of
life is to give it away.

—*David Viscott*

SEPTEMBER 19

Each golden sunrise ushers in new opportunities for those who retain faith in themselves, and keep their chins up. No one has ever seen a cock crow with its head down... Meet the sunrise with confidence.

—Alonzo Newton Benn

SEPTEMBER 20

All the wonders you seek are within yourself.

—Sir Thomas Browne

Some pursue happiness—
others **CREATE** it.

—Ralph Waldo Emerson

SEPTEMBER 22

Like a welcome summer rain, humor may suddenly cleanse and cool the earth, the air, and you.

—*Langston Hughes*

SEPTEMBER 23

Don't curse the darkness—light a candle.

—*Chinese Proverb*

SEPTEMBER 24

Success is not the key to happiness. Happiness is the key to success. If you love what you are doing, you will be successful.

—*Albert Schweitzer*

SEPTEMBER 25

There are some people who live in a dream world, and there are some who face reality; and then there are those who turn one into the other.

—*Douglas H. Everett*

SEPTEMBER 26

Those people who think they know everything are a great annoyance to those of us who do.

—*Isaac Asimov*

SEPTEMBER 27

The happiness of your life depends upon the quality of your thoughts.

—*Marcus Aurelius*

SEPTEMBER 28

Find what makes your heart sing, and create your own music.

—Mac Anderson

SEPTEMBER 29

All our dreams can come true, if we have the courage to pursue them.

—Walt Disney

SEPTEMBER 30

Don't aim for success if you want it; just do what you love and believe in, and it will come naturally.

—David Frost

What is the difference between an obstacle and an opportunity? Our attitude toward it. Every opportunity has a difficulty, and every difficulty has an OPPORTUNITY.

—*J. Sidlow Baxter*

OCTOBER 2

Life is change. Growth is optional. Choose wisely.

—Karen Kaiser Clark

OCTOBER 3

As we let our own light shine, we unconsciously give other people permission to do the same.

—Marianne Williamson

OCTOBER 4

To improve the golden moment of opportunity, and catch the good that is within our reach, is the great art of life.

—Samuel Johnson

OCTOBER 5

Life's ups and downs provide windows of opportunity to determine your values and goals. Think of using all obstacles as stepping stones to build the life you want.

—*Marsha Sinetar*

OCTOBER 6

You are today where your thoughts have brought you; you will be tomorrow where your thoughts take you.

—*James Lane Allen*

OCTOBER 7

Thought is the sculptor who can create the person you want to be.

—*Henry David Thoreau*

OCTOBER 8

Do your work with your whole heart and you will succeed—there's so little competition.

—*Elbert Hubbard*

OCTOBER 9

Today is your day and mine, the only day we have, the day in which we play our part. What our part may signify in the great whole we may not understand, but we are here to play it, and now is the TIME.

—*David Starr Jordan*

OCTOBER 10

Happiness depends upon ourselves.

—*Aristotle*

Those who are lifting the world upward and onward are those who encourage more than criticize.

—Elizabeth Harrison

The Constitution only gives people the right to pursue happiness. You have to catch it yourself.

—Benjamin Franklin

There is no exercise better for the heart than reaching down and lifting people up.

—John Holmes

OCTOBER 14

A smile of encouragement at the right moment may act like sunlight on a closed-up flower; it may be the turning point for a struggling life.

—*Alfred A. Montapert*

OCTOBER 15

We cannot hold a torch to light another's path without brightening our own.

—*Ben Sweetland*

OCTOBER 16

An effort made for the happiness of others lifts us above ourselves.

—*Lydia Maria Child*

Start by doing what's necessary; then do what's possible; and suddenly you are doing the impossible.

—*Saint Francis of Assisi*

An optimist is a fellow who believes a housefly is looking for a way to get out.

—*George Jean Nathan*

Your present circumstances don't determine where you can go; they merely determine where you start.

—*Nido Qubein*

OCTOBER 20

Love is the only force capable of transforming an enemy to a FRIEND.

—*Martin Luther King Jr.*

Action may not always bring happiness, but there is no happiness without action.

—*Benjamin Disraeli*

The way to happiness: keep your heart free from hate, your mind from worry. Live simply, expect little, give much. Scatter sunshine, forget self, think of others.

—*Norman Vincent Peale*

OCTOBER 23

We ourselves feel that what we are doing is just a drop in the ocean. But the ocean would be less because of that missing drop.

—*Mother Teresa*

OCTOBER 24

You can give without loving, but you can never love without giving.

—*Robert Louis Stevenson*

OCTOBER 25

Live as if you were to die tomorrow. Learn as if you were to live forever.

—*Mahatma Gandhi*

OCTOBER 26

Happiness is not a goal; it is a by-product of a life well lived.

—Eleanor Roosevelt

OCTOBER 27

The ideals which have lighted my way, and time after time have given me new courage to face life cheerfully, have been Kindness, Beauty, and Truth.

—Albert Einstein

OCTOBER 28

Some cause happiness wherever they go; others, whenever they go.

—Oscar Wilde

OCTOBER 29

The greatest glory in living lies not in never falling, but in rising every time we fall.

—*Nelson Mandela*

OCTOBER 30

Carve your name on hearts, not on marble.

—*Charles H. Spurgeon*

OCTOBER 31

The root of joy is gratefulness... It is not joy that makes us grateful; it is gratitude that makes us joyful.

—*David Steindl-Rast*

NOVEMBER 1

When one door of happiness closes, another opens; but often we look so long at the closed door that we do not see the one which has been opened for us.

—*Helen Keller*

Taking joy in living is a woman's best cosmetic.

—*Rosalind Russell*

The essence of life is not in the great victories and grand failures, but in the simple joys.

—*Jonathan Lockwood Huie*

To me, every hour of the day and night is an unspeakably perfect miracle.

—*Walt Whitman*

NOVEMBER 5

Anything done for another is done for oneself.

—*Pope John Paul II*

NOVEMBER 6

An optimist is a person who sees a green light everywhere, while the pessimist sees only the red stoplight. The truly wise person is color-blind.

—*Albert Schweitzer*

NOVEMBER 7

If a man does his best, what else is there?

—*George S. Patton*

NOVEMBER 8

Keep your eyes on the stars, and your feet on the ground.

—Theodore Roosevelt

NOVEMBER 9

It's what you learn after you know it all that counts.

—John Wooden

NOVEMBER 10

We are here to change the world with small acts of thoughtfulness done daily rather than with one great breakthrough.

—Rabbi Harold Kushner

If you think you're too small to have an impact, try going to bed with a mosquito.

—*Anita Roddick*

Life will bring you pain all by itself. Your responsibility is to create joy.

—*Milton Erickson*

When it comes to life, the critical thing is whether you take things for granted or take them with gratitude.

—*Gilbert K. Chesterton*

NOVEMBER 14

All that is worth cherishing begins in the heart,
not in the head.

—Suzanne Chapin

NOVEMBER 15

The power to affect your future lies within your own hands.

—Nido Qubein

NOVEMBER 16

A strong positive mental attitude will create more
miracles than any wonder drug.

—Patricia Neal

NOVEMBER 17

If you walk in joy, happiness is close behind.

—Todd Stocker

NOVEMBER 18

You have within you, right now, everything you need to deal with whatever the world can throw at you.

—Brian Tracy

NOVEMBER 19

Though no one can go back and make a brand-new start, anyone can start from now and make a brand-new ending.

—Carl Bard

NOVEMBER 20

Happiness is an inside Job.

—*William Arthur Ward*

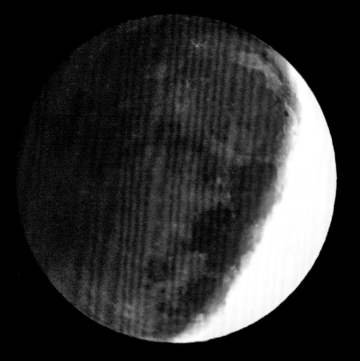

When I started counting my blessings, my whole life turned AROUND.

—*Willie Nelson*

NOVEMBER 22

You are always only one choice away from changing your life.

—Mary Blochowiak

NOVEMBER 23

If we don't change, we don't grow. If we don't grow, we aren't really living.

—Gail Sheehy

NOVEMBER 24

We enjoy warmth because we have been cold. We appreciate light because we have been in darkness. By the same token, we can experience joy because we have known sadness.

—David Weatherford

NOVEMBER 25

The only question in life is whether or not you are going to answer a hearty "yes!" to your adventure.

—*Joseph Campbell*

NOVEMBER 26

Life is a great big canvas, and you should throw all the paint on it you can.

—*Danny Kaye*

NOVEMBER 27

Find ecstasy in life; the mere sense of living is joy enough.

—*Emily Dickinson*

NOVEMBER 28

The key to success in life is using the good thoughts of wise people.

—Leo Tolstoy

NOVEMBER 29

When you arise in the morning, think of what a precious privilege it is to be alive—to breathe, to think, to enjoy, to love.

—Marcus Aurelius

NOVEMBER 30

The noblest pleasure is the joy of understanding.

—Leonardo da Vinci

In times of *JOY*, all of us wished
we possessed a tail we could wag.

—*W. H. Auden*

Life is what we make it, always has been, always will be.

—Grandma Moses

The world is but a canvas to our imagination.

—Henry David Thoreau

We must not allow the clock and the calendar to blind us to the fact that each moment of life is a miracle and mystery.

—H. G. Wells

DECEMBER 5

The smallest change in perspective can transform a life. What tiny attitude adjustment might turn your world around?

—*Oprah Winfrey*

DECEMBER 6

Joy blooms where minds and hearts are open.

—*Jonathan Lockwood Huie*

DECEMBER 7

People say that what we're all seeking is a meaning for life... I think that what we're seeking is the experience of being alive...

—*Joseph Campbell*

DECEMBER 8

Inner peace can be reached only
when we practice FORGIVENESS.

—*Gerald Jampolsky*

DECEMBER 9

Be content with what you have; rejoice in the way things are. When you realize there is nothing lacking, the whole world belongs to you.

—Lao Tzu

DECEMBER 10

Once you make a decision, the universe conspires to make it happen.

—Ralph Waldo Emerson

DECEMBER 11

Joy weathers any storm:
happiness rides the waves.

—*Todd Stocker*

DECEMBER 12

Develop an attitude of gratitude and give thanks for
everything that happens to you, knowing that every
step forward is a step toward achieving something
bigger and better than your current situation.

—*Brian Tracy*

There is no beautifier of complexion, or form, or behavior, like the wish to scatter joy and not pain around us.

—*Ralph Waldo Emerson*

DECEMBER 14

To enjoy your life most of the time, you've got to realize that the world hasn't been doing it to you! You've been doing it to yourself.

—*Ken Keyes Jr.*

DECEMBER 15

Life shrinks or expands in proportion to one's courage.

—*Anaïs Nin*

DECEMBER 16

A happy life must be to a great extent a quiet life, for it is only in an atmosphere of quiet that true joy dare live.

—Bertrand Russell

DECEMBER 17

Slow down and enjoy life. It's not only the scenery you miss by going too fast—you also miss the sense of where you are going and why.

—Eddie Cantor

DECEMBER 18

The greatest use of life is to spend it for something that will outlast it.

—*William James*

DECEMBER 19

Have you had a kindness shown?

Pass it on;

'Twas not given for thee alone,

Pass it on;

Let it travel down the years,

Let it wipe another's tears,

Till in Heaven the deed appears—

Pass it on.

—*Henry Burton*

DECEMBER 20

When the heart is full of joy,
it allows its joy to escape...
The only full heart is the
overflowing ♡EART.

—*Charles Spurgeon*

DECEMBER 21

The important thing is not how many years in your life but how much life in your years.

—*Edward Stieglitz*

DECEMBER 22

Let there be more joy and laughter in your living.

—*Eileen Caddy*

DECEMBER 23

How wonderful it is that nobody need wait a single moment before starting to improve the world.

—*Anne Frank*

DECEMBER 24

It is not true that people stop pursuing dreams because they grow old, they grow old because they stop pursuing dreams.

—*Gabriel García Márquez*

DECEMBER 25

If you don't like something, change it. If you can't change it, change your attitude.

—*Maya Angelou*

DECEMBER 26

The most wasted of all days is one without laughter.

—*E. E. Cummings*

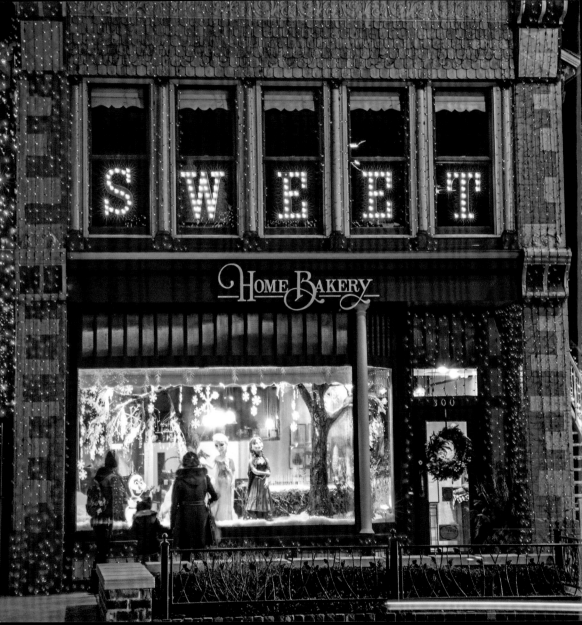

DECEMBER 27

I never lose sight of the fact that just being is fun.

—*Katharine Hepburn*

DECEMBER 28

One can never consent to creep when one feels an impulse to soar.

—*Helen Keller*

DECEMBER 29

I have always been delighted at the prospect of a new day, a fresh try, one more start, with perhaps a bit of magic waiting somewhere behind the morning.

—*J. B. Priestley*

Joy does not simply happen to us. We have to choose joy and keep choosing it every day.

—*Henri J. M. Nouwen*

One must put all the happiness one can into each moment.

—*Edith Wharton*

ABOUT THE AUTHOR

Mac Anderson is the founder of Simple Truths and Successories, Inc., the leader in designing and marketing products for motivation and recognition. However, these companies are not the first success stories for Mac. He was also the founder and CEO of McCord Travel, the largest travel company in the Midwest, and part owner/ vice president of sales and marketing for the Orval Kent Company, the country's largest manufacturer of prepared salads.

His accomplishments in these unrelated industries provide some insight into his passion and leadership skills. He also brings the same passion in his speaking engagements to many corporate audiences on a variety of topics including leadership, motivation, and team building.

Mac has authored or coauthored twenty-five books that have sold more than four million copies.

- *212° Leadership*
- *212° The Extra Degree*
- *212° Service*
- *Best of Success*
- *Change Is Good... You Go First*
- *Charging the Human Battery*
- *Customer Love*
- *The Dash*
- *The Essence of Leadership*
- *Even Eagles Need a Push*
- *Finding Joy*
- *Habits Die Hard*
- *Leadership Quotes*
- *Learning to Dance in the Rain*
- *Motivational Quotes*
- *The Nature of Success*
- *One Choice*
- *The Power of Attitude*
- *The Power of Kindness*
- *The Road to Happiness*
- *The Secret of Living Is Giving*
- *Things That Grab Your Heart and Won't Let Go*
- *To a Child, Love Is Spelled T-I-M-E*
- *What's the Big Idea?*
- *You Can't Send a Duck to Eagle School*

Todd Reed has photographed the beauty of Michigan for more than four decades, first as a photojournalist for his hometown newspaper, the *Ludington Daily News*, then as one of Michigan's best known outdoor photographers.

Brad Reed, Todd's son, is an international award-winning outdoor photographer. The Calvin College graduate left teaching when he realized his passion for photography was as strong as his father's.

Todd and Brad's artwork has been featured by Nikon and the North American Photography Association and in many publications, including *Michigan BLUE* and *Traverse* magazines. Their work has been exhibited around the state, as well as in the international ArtPrize exhibition in Grand Rapids. Their Michigan imagery is often seen on billboards across the state and the Midwest to promote Michigan travel.

Together, Todd and Brad own and operate one of the finest photography galleries in the country, the Todd and Brad Reed Photo

Gallery in downtown Ludington. The lifelong Michigan residents are actively involved in their community and are passionate about their beloved hometown and the state of Michigan.

Brad lives in downtown Ludington with his two kids, Julia and Ethan.

Todd and his wife, Debbie, live near the Lake Michigan shoreline in Ludington. They have three sons, Tad, Brad, and Willie; two daughters-in-law, Misty and Stephanie; and six grandchildren, Rachel, Julia, Ty, Austin, Ethan, and Tucker.

For more information about the images in this book, visit their website at ToddandBradReed.com.